Table of Contents

The Best in Me

God, bested me
My heart, couldn't rest you see?
Because He tested me
My mind messed with me
I wasn't impressed with He
Evil was possessed in me
But God, He was obsessed with me
-Why? Why was He obsessed with me?
Because God saw the best in me
My heart can rest you see?
Because He tested me
My mind is blessed by thee
My heart is possessed by He
I! I am obsessed with thee
And God? He is impressed with me
Because God tested me

Easy I Shall Rest

The ground I am lowered into
6 feet below, I paid my due
A life of service and sacrifice
Just like my Savior Jesus Christ
A lot of paths to get me here
Around me all the people I hold dear
Some paths went astray
But I believed in Him this day
I did my best
Easy I shall rest

End of Mission

In the field we look for a lost ring
This part sure does sting
A comrade has passed
That mission was his last
In the truck sits a gunner
A bomb went off like thunder
A comrade had paid his due
His mission is now through
There sits a team of three
Just hit by a 1000 lb HME
Three comrades it did beat
Their mission is now complete
Many comrades have departed
But my battle just started
Now I sit here just wishin'
It was my end of mission

The Other Side

I wish I knew what it's like to be dead
Watch people laugh and listen to what they said
Observe them mourn
For this soul that is scorn
Watch the ones that once loved me
As they forget about me quickly
See them laugh and play
They forgot about me anyway
But the fighting I will continue
I only wish they knew
How badly this lost soul needs saved
To Jesus I talked and prayed
But happiness I will continue to seek
In this life that is so bleak

My First Prayer

On my knees here I'm praying
I figured I'd just start saying
Dear God, I'm sorry that on you I turned my back
You have to understand, you've cut me no slack

You've challenged me but kept me in your hand
Knowing there is nothing I can't withstand
You've always been in my heart
And I've known that from the start

Now I kneel to you in these prison stripes
Please, dear God, will I be alright?
It may be too late but I ask you please
As I sit here sobbing on my knees

Dear God, please listen to my story
I now choose to live in your glory
Off my knees, I will stand
Dear God, my life is in your hands

Struggle with Faith

All dressed up with no place to go
Layeth an atheist 6 feet below
Never accepting God in his heart
That was the mistake from the start

Wearing the wings for an eternity
Lives a Christian who accepted thee
Wandering the streets paved with gold
Walks a believer never to grow old

God works in mysterious ways
Believe and accept him throughout your days
Live a life that you can cherish
God will accept you when you perish

The Change in Me

My smile could light up a room
My laughter was heard like a boom
My thoughts were clear
My loved ones were near
My jokes made people laugh
But that was only the good half
Now my smile is bleak
My laughter is weak
My thoughts are dark
My loved ones I pushed too far
My jokes are no more
This is not what I was intended for

Dues Paid

Stand at attention soldier!
This war isn't over
Salute the men you've lost
Only you know the cost

Stand at parade rest soldier!
This war isn't over
A comrade has departed
But this fight has only started

Stand at ease soldier!
Your war is now over
Your comrades cry for you
For you have paid your due

Queen of Battle

I was in the Infantry
Fought with honor and bravery
Pick up my gun and look down the sight
We were the first to fight
Infantry, stubborn to the core
They trained us for war
But never to come home
Now I sit here and write this poem
This is how I cope
I had so little hope
Now, I'm in a different fight
Struggling with all my might
Post-traumatic stress disorder
My mind is a hoarder
These thoughts I can never let go
It burns me to my soul
I was in the Infantry
I fought for my country
Now, I write this poetry

Anxiety

In this room many people gather
Alone, I would be rather
All of these people laughing I see
A smile comes on the face of me
Feeling like a lost cause
Remembering all that was
The blood, the sweat, the war
In my head, I keep it in the store
I am screaming silently
My thoughts appear violently
My heart begins to pound
I can barely feel the ground
A deep breath I take
This anxiety I can't fake

No One Understands

She said "Think thoughts that are happy"
No, not dark and sappy
It's happy thoughts I should write
But happiness is out of sight
I can't write about glee
A smile never comes on the face of me
"Remember the times that were good"
If it didn't make me cry I would
It's happiness that I miss
As I stay in this dark abyss
Thoughts of laughter I could share
Instead I write thoughts that scare
I try to picture my last breath
And it scares me to death

Never Forgotten

My mind races
I remember the faces
Men dying in front of me
Their tears I could see
An army of one
Their time is done
Army strong
This night is long
Always a soldier
Til their fight is over
Til Valhalla I pray
I remember them every day

Clinched Hands

I clinch my hands together
With Christ, this I can weather
My prayers are quiet
With Christ, I can't hide it
I tell Him my short little story
With Christ, looking out for me
Around me is His essence
With Christ, he's always present
My story will be told
With Christ, I will walk the golden road

Continued Fight

My mind is easy with integrity
My heart rests peacefully with honesty
I am a simple man with a troubled past
Struggling in the darkness that is vast
I am surviving with this disease
Have mercy on me please
PTSD has gotten the best of me
It has knocked me to my knees
I will stand and continue to fight
Until this darkness is out of sight

Every Time

Every time I tried
My mind it lied
My heart it cried
Every time I tried
My spirit it died
My mouth it dried
Every time I tried
Rationale never applied
In my thoughts I'd hide
Every time I tried
My feelings were amplified
My eyes were wide
This gun was by my side
Every time I tried
To commit suicide

PTSD

Anger and Hostility
It's what's instilled in me
Our country tis of thee
I fought for lady liberty
I went to Iraq
Now I'm back
Off to Afghanistan
Look I'm back again
Stress and Anxiety
It's what's inside of me
Oh say can't you see
I did it for lady liberty
I can't handle this infection
I lost my complexion
Don't recognize my reflection
Just one more injection
Depression and Misery
It's what lives in me
I did it for lady liberty
But she turned her back to me
I remember the dead
The obituaries I read
Why not me instead?
Anger and Hostility

It's what's instilled in me
Stress and Anxiety
It's what's inside of me
Depression and Misery
It's what lives in me
Our country tis of thee
Oh say can't you see
I did it for liberty
This, this is PTSD

Talk to Me!

I don't need medication you see?
I need someone to talk to me
My heart and mind they hurt
With death I always flirt

I choose life that is what I desire
Fulfill my destiny, that is what I admire
This life has been rough
Living with this disease has been tough

Struggling to stay in this fight
I finally see the light
It is with him I worship and praise
I will follow in his ways

Sit down and let me talk
In my boots you can take a walk
My mind I will try to get you to realize
Just what I've seen with my two eyes
Living in this disguise

S-U-I-C-I-D-E

<u>S</u>urely you can,
<u>U</u>nderstand this is tough
<u>I</u> have been crying
<u>C</u>aring was not enough
<u>I</u>nside I've been dying
<u>D</u>eath doesn't seem so rough
<u>E</u>ven my thoughts are lying

The Forgotten Soldier

I served my country before
I fought and bled in war
Help to the wounded and dead
Wishing it were me instead
My life I would sacrifice
So these men could live twice
Soldiers knocking on a mom's door
Her son died in this war
A wife falls to her knees
These uniformed men try to keep her at ease
I didn't die in the war
No one will knock on my door
I will die because of PTSD
No one will remember me

Unofficial Army Song

First to cry in the night
For we've lost another fight
And the soldier is crying alone
Proud of all he has done
Ne'er is the battle won
And the soldier is struggling alone
And it's hi, hi, hey!
A soldier has lost his way
Count off another lost at war!
For wherever he goes
You will always know
A soldier is marching alone!

Served with Honor

On top of his casket
Layeth the flag
In it a man wouldn't brag
The union over his chest
We shall lay this man to rest
Carried off into the plane
Is a man who was slain
Lowered into the ground
You only hear one sound
A widow you hear cry
For she lost this remarkable guy

It's Okay to Cry

Trapped in this cell
I'm living in hell
My mind is lying
I am slowly dying
Once, my life was great
Now this trigger will decide my fate
A deep breath I take
"Pull the trigger for goodness sake"
Afraid to live, scared to die…
I'll just sit here and cry

Carry On

My heart is pounding
In my thoughts I'm drowning
My chest is tight
My breath is light
My ears are ringing
I hear the angels are singing
But the demons they are screaming
I must be dreaming
My throat is dry
I continue to cry
I do not want to die
Not today!
Not this way!
I must wait!
To determine my fate

Life of Strife

On this bed so stale
I live in hell
Tears fall from my eye
Every day I cry
I tried to do well in life
But I've caused so much strife
I turned my back on Christ
Even though it was his life that was sacrificed
Now I lay on this hard bed
I talk to him instead
To Jesus I try to speak
But my prayers are weak
I try to read between the lines
I'm always looking for signs
Now the signs I have read
I listened to what Jesus said
His words are gentle and stern
On this bed so firm

Going Well

Why do I believe in God? Well,
I've already lived through hell
A life of torment and sacrifice
That was our savior Jesus Christ

From the cross our savior hang
Listen closely as the angels sang
Soon rising from his grave
Our lives he will save

Trials and tests there will be
Follow Christ and listen to me
For I've already lived through hell
But with him, things are going well

Soon

My life, I started to waste
Actions, I began to decide in a haste
Death began to stare me in the face
Fighting to stay alive
This is how I'd survive
My own life, I'd live deprived
Soon, I'll begin to thrive
PTSD won't keep up pace
For so long, I've felt displaced
Death, will sheepishly look into my face
I will continue to be graced
For it is happiness I will chase
My comrades I will embrace

I Gave All

Everything, to you, I gave it all
I tried to answer your every call
The late nights and early morning
I was left without a warning
No opportunity to converse
You left, but what's worse?
You left in stride
You were able to push it all aside
Pick up like I was never there
Be free, as if, you never cared
Perhaps I will move on
But my feelings for you, will never be gone
I will seek to find peace
But you left me with such ease
Now, more damaged than before
I will continue to fight this war
A fight you never would understand
Because I worried, every time I held your hand

I Wish You Understood

Nobody knows the struggles I felt
The pain and torment I have been dealt
I thought I was beating my disease
As it crumpled me to my knees
I was always there for you
But I didn't know, how bad I needed it too
I thought, my demons, I could beat
But I'd eventually accept defeat
I began to self harm
But, I never sounded the alarm
I stayed silent
My head became violent
The darkness just continued to last
My heart began to crash
Life came at me too fast
I didn't know how I got here
All I knew is I always had fear
I felt I was never good enough
Here! Take all this stuff!
I was crippled by my mind!
I said it all the time!
In words you never understood
But, I said them I just thought you could

Therapy Assignment

Goodbye, I say goodbye to suicide
You made me think I'd be better but you lied
Death was not a better plan
Life is better, let me make you understand
I lived so long in misery and despair
But it's time to clear the air
I am worth living my best life
You already made me lose my wife
You left me crippled and alone
You took everything and now, I'm on my own
Fuck you suicide, you don't own me
I am better off let me be
You were so close I could taste it
My life would have been wasted
The rest of my life is still unwritten
So now, I will break tradition
Suicide, you don't give a fuck
You took advantage of me when I was down on my luck
Listen to me, listen to this suicide
Here I am! Let me confide
I will stand here and smile
You owned me for such a long while
The gun in my mouth
Or into traffic heading south

You will not take me from this world
You will not take me from my boy and girl
You are greedy and conceited
But I will not be defeated
So I say goodbye to you suicide
I know you wish I would've died

Therapy Assignment (Round Two)

Cultivating my mental health
Establishing my mental wealth
This place, me they will treat
I struggle and I cry but I won't be beat
Everyone around me is an acquaintance
But I will work on my own maintenance
In this bed I lay
Everything taken away
My demons I will combat
I will win, that is that
Accompany me and we will succeed
Our demons won't impede
So long as we work on our mental health
We will build our mental wealth

One is Too Many

Let me tell you something true
I am close to becoming 1 of 22
I lay with dark thoughts in the night
A future I see nowhere in sight
I promise I'll keep trying
It's is rough though, always crying
I have lost everything- lost it all
Here I lay crying- about to take the fall
I have done all the treatment I can
This feels so impossible, just being one man
I got your six and I'll be there for you
I'll just be gone and 1 of 22

My Apologies

I am sorry mother
I tried to be a good brother
I was a good father
To my son and daughter
Mother I must say sorry to you
I did all I could do
I kept trying to fight
I did—with all my might
I struggled and I prayed
But I continued to be afraid
When, for the last time my eyes close
Just remember momma this is not what I chose
I love you, and my sisters too
Tell my kids I said "I love you"
This won't be merely a vacation
Because I have reached my final destination